A BEACON BIOGRAPHY

Robert Griffin III

RG3

Pete DiPrimio

PURPLE TOAD
PUBLISHING

P.O. Box 631
Kennett Square, Pennsylvania 19348
www.purpletoadpublishing.com

Printing   1   2   3   4   5   6   7   8   9

A Beacon Biography

Big Time Rush
Carly Rae Jepsen
Drake
Harry Styles of One Direction
Jennifer Lawrence
Kevin Durant
Robert Griffin III (RG3)

Publisher's Cataloging-in-Publication Data
DiPrimio, Pete
    Robert Griffin III / Pete DiPrimio
        p. cm. – (A beacon biography)
Includes bibliographic references and index.
ISBN: 978-1-62469-021-1 (library bound)
1. Griffin, Robert, III, 1990– — 2. Football players—United States—Biography—Juvenile literature. I. Title.
 GV939.G7544 2013
 796.332092—dc23
                                                                            2013934693

eBook ISBN: 9781624690280

ABOUT THE AUTHOR: Pete DiPrimio is an award-winning Indiana sports writer, a veteran children's author, and a long-time freelance writer. He's also a journalism adjunct lecturer and fitness instructor.

Printed by Lake Book Manufacturing, Chicago, IL

CONTENTS

Washington rookie quarterback Robert Griffin III took his share of big hits late in the season, and they finally caught up to him in a playoff loss to Seattle.

Risk and Reward

Robert Griffin III lay crumpled facedown on the battered grass of Washington's FedEx Field. Suddenly, a promising NFL future was in doubt.

Griffin was the Washington Redskins' outstanding rookie quarterback. He was fast, athletic, and had a strong arm. He hurt teams with his running and passing. The National Football League (NFL) had chosen him as the no. 2 overall draft pick, and he'd been awarded the Heisman Trophy from Baylor University. Much was expected of him, and so far, he had delivered.

Griffin had led the Redskins to the playoffs. They had won seven straight games after a 3–6 start to win the NFC East title. He had done things few quarterbacks had ever done before— throwing for 3,200 yards and 20 touchdowns, rushing for 815 yards and seven touchdowns.

But an injury—a mild right knee sprain—had robbed him of some of his speed and mobility. He wore a big brace, but playing was still risky. Professional football is a tough game. Players are bigger, faster, and stronger than ever before. Would it be better for coach Mike Shanahan to hold him out and let the knee heal?

But these were the NFL playoffs, and Griffin wanted to play. His team needed him. He wasn't about to give in to a little pain. He was tougher than that.

The Seattle Seahawks had hit him hard throughout this wildcard playoff game. One first-quarter hit left him limping badly. It was his right knee, the one he'd hurt a month earlier against the Baltimore Ravens after getting hit by defensive tackle Haloti Ngata.

Early on against Seattle, Griffin was on fire. He took Washington to a 14–0 lead. But after the hit, he wasn't the same, and neither were the Redskins. Some wondered if backup quarterback Kirk Cousins should replace him, but no change was made.

"You respect authority, and I respect Coach Shanahan," Griffin said after the game. "But at the same time, you have to step up and be a man, sometimes. There was no way I was coming out of that game."

"I think I did put myself at more risk by being out there," he said later. "But every time you get on the field, you're putting yourself on the line."

In the fourth quarter, with Washington trailing and struggling to score, Griffin slipped trying to get a bad shotgun snap. His right knee buckled, although later, team officials would say he was hurt on the previous play.

In the end, it didn't matter. Griffin's season was over. In a few minutes, so was Washington's. Seattle won 24–14.

Some blamed the FedEx Field playing conditions for Griffin's injury. The grass was torn up and players were constantly slipping on it. Seattle coach Pete Carroll told a Seattle radio station it was "a horrible field" and "we deserve better."

Fans and media were upset. Why take the risk with so young and promising a quarterback? Coach Shanahan took most of the

Despite the fact that Coach Shanahan has won two Super Bowl championships during his career, some fans blamed him for Griffin's further injury after playing him in the game against Seattle.

heat. Was he more interested in winning than in the health of his star player?

Shanahan told the *NFL Network* that team doctors had cleared Griffin to play. He said, "You'd have to be a complete idiot to think I would overrule our doctors. That's ludicrous. If someone were to do that, they should be fired."

Griffin defended his coach and his own decision to play with a couple of tweets: "Many may question, criticize & think they have all the right answers. But few have been in the line of fire in battle."

He added: "I thank God for perspective and because of that I appreciate the support from everyone. I also appreciate the criticism."

Dr. James Andrews, an orthopedic surgeon, would see what the damage was and what could be done to fix it. Griffin was young and strong. He would get the best medical care and rehabilitation.

Still, the question lingered—would he be the same player?

Robert Griffin III is ready to have a long, outstanding career with the Washington Redskins.

Robert Griffin III grew up working hard. He had no choice. It was the family way—starting with his grandfather, Robert Griffin, a tough-as-nails construction worker from New Orleans.

Griffin III was born on February 12, 1990, in Okinawa, Japan, to military parents. His father, Robert Griffin II, spent 21 years in the U.S. Army. He was a petroleum specialist who retired as sergeant first class. His mother, Jacqueline, had reached the level of sergeant in the army. She had served for 12 years.

Discipline was a big deal in the Griffin house. So was religion. Griffin III and his two older sisters, Jihan and Dejan, understood the importance of doing things right and well. If you started something, you finished it. You were polite. You were consistent and hard working. "Yes, sir" and "No, ma'am" were part of your vocabulary.

They grew up on the move. The Army sent the Griffins to Japan, South Korea, Fort Carson (Colorado), Fort Lewis (Washington), and Fort Hood (Texas). For a while, when their parents were stationed in South Korea, Griffin III and his sisters

Robert Griffin III and his father, Robert Griffin II

lived with their grandparents in New Orleans. When their parents returned, the family settled in Copperas Cove, Texas, near Fort Hood.

Back then, he was known as "Little Robert." His famous nickname, "RG3," came years later from a TV sportscaster in Waco, Texas, while Griffin III was in college.

Griffin II was set to retire from the army, but on Griffin III's thirteenth birthday, his father was sent to the war in Iraq. Griffin II didn't want his son to worry, so he told him not to watch TV about the war. He promised to call home often, and he did.

Griffin II returned home in December 2003 and finally retired. He eventually earned a bachelor's degree and a master's degree from Texas A&M, and then became a psychological counselor at Fort Hood.

Early on, Griffin III's big sport was basketball. He was a huge fan of NBA superstar Michael Jordan. He didn't start playing organized football until he was 11. He also ran track and quickly became one of the nation's fastest hurdlers in his age group.

Griffin was a very quiet boy who saved his allowance money

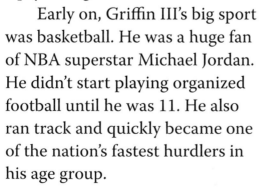

Griffin II and Jacqueline Griffin

Griffin was a state champion in hurdles.

for things he really wanted or needed. His parents had these rules—homework came first, good grades got you extra allowance or toys, and teenagers didn't need their own cars.

Griffin's favorite toys were Batman, Power Rangers, and Teenage Mutant Ninja Turtles. He liked to wear colorful socks that had turtles or *SpongeBob SquarePants* TV characters on them.

Griffin II and Jacqueline helped train their son for sports. His father became an AAU youth track coach who worked out his son based on military intensity, discipline, and planning. The message was clear—hard work will beat talent if talent doesn't work hard.

Jacqueline videotaped every practice. Griffin's parents would go over the tapes with him, and then show him videos of successful NFL quarterbacks and Olympic champions.

Griffin was on the football, basketball, and track teams at Copperas Cove High School. Many of his workouts came after football practice. Sometimes he'd pull a tire—a training technique that improves a runner's strength and endurance. He would tie a rope to an old tire, and then attach the other end of the rope to a

Few high school football players were faster than Griffin. As a senior, he set two Texas state track records, and was ranked no. 1 nationally in his age group in the 110- and 300-meter hurdles.

wide belt on his waist. As he ran, the tire would drag flat on the ground behind him. He'd also train by running up hills on his way home from school.

By the time he was a senior, big-time colleges such as Stanford, Tennessee, Kansas, Nebraska, Houston, Illinois, Oregon, and Washington wanted Griffin as a football player. In his two years as the starting quarterback at Copperas Cove, he threw for 3,357 yards and 41 touchdowns while rushing for more than 2,100 yards for 32 touchdowns. As a senior he led Copperas Cove to a Texas state runner-up finish and a 13–2 record. Rivals. com, a national Internet recruiting service, rated him as the nation's no. 3 dual-threat (run and pass) quarterback.

Other colleges wanted him for track. Griffin set state records in the 110- and 300-meter hurdle races. In 2007, he was ranked no. 1 nationally in his age group in both hurdle races. He was fast enough to qualify for the 2008 Olympic Trials in the 400-meter hurdles.

Griffin was also very smart. He became the Copperas Cove senior class president and graduated seventh in his class after the first semester of his senior year.

All this could have made him cocky. Instead, he was very humble and thankful, especially to his teammates who helped him become successful. Griffin always credited God for giving him the ability to make it possible. He'd show his offensive linemen appreciation by bringing them donuts.

A lot of colleges thought Griffin would be a better wide receiver or running back, but he wanted to play quarterback. Tennessee made his final list. So did Stanford, whose coach was the popular Jim Harbaugh.

Houston coach Art Briles made a big push to sign Griffin. That continued when Briles took over the Baylor program in Waco, Texas. It also helped that Baylor had a powerhouse track program under coach Clyde Hart, who had coached former Olympic gold medalist Michael Johnson. Griffin wanted to be on both teams.

In the end, he decided that Stanford was too far, and Tennessee was too uncertain. Griffin would be a Baylor Bear.

Many colleges fiercely recruited Griffin. In the end, he chose Baylor University, a Christian college that was only about 70 miles from his Copperas Cove, Texas, home.

Before Griffin arrived, Baylor had never beaten Oklahoma. As a junior, he led the Bears to an upset victory over the no. 5 Sooners.

College Opportunity

Griffin was just seventeen years old when he enrolled at Baylor in January 2008. He went through Baylor's winter workouts for football and track, and then spring football practice and track meets. In track he won the Big 12 conference 400 hurdle race and placed third in the NCAA meet to earn All-America honors.

That summer he competed in the U.S. Olympic Trials, but did not advance to the finals and did not make the Olympic team.

The football competition was tough considering veteran quarterback Blake Szymanski was back, along with a transfer from the University of Miami, Kirby Freeman. But by the second game of his freshman season, Griffin had become the starter.

He made an instant impact. He set an NCAA record by starting his career without throwing an interception in his first 209 passes. He was impressive enough to win Big 12 freshman of the year honors even though Baylor went just 4–8. Griffin was so good that some people talked about him transferring to a better football program. He wasn't interested. He was happy being a Baylor Bear.

Early in his sophomore season, Griffin tore up his knee and had to miss the rest of the games. But he came back strong the next year, 2010, and led Baylor to a 7–6 record while throwing for 3,501 yards.

In 2011, Griffin became nationally known as "RG3," a 6-foot-2, 220-pound force of football nature. He threw for 4,293 yards, 37 touchdowns, and just six interceptions. He also rushed for 699 yards and 10 touchdowns. Griffin led Baylor to a 10–3 record—tying the school record for wins set in 1980—and an Alamo Bowl victory over Washington.

At times, he was almost too good to believe. Griffin made a 15-yard catch on a third-down-and-10-yards-to-go play that led to the winning field goal in a 50–48 win over no. 16 Texas Christian University (TCU). He threw for 479 yards, including the scrambling, game-winning 34-yard touchdown pass with eight seconds left to beat no. 5 Oklahoma 45–38. It was Baylor's first win over Oklahoma in college football history.

Griffin's ability to run as well as pass made him the no. 1 target of every defense. More and more colleges are recruiting dual-threat quarterbacks like him.

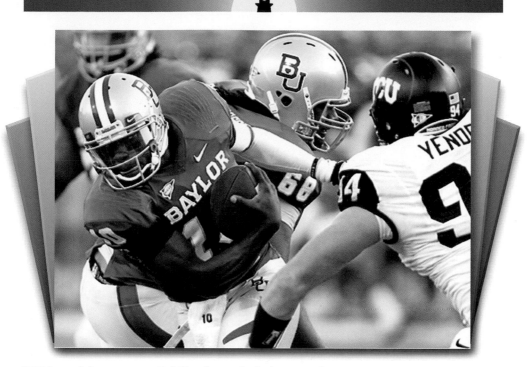

TCU could not stop Griffin from helping Baylor upset Texas 50–48.

Griffin won a slew of awards, including All-America and Academic All-America. He won the Davey O'Brien Award, which annually goes to the nation's best quarterback.

"He epitomizes everything you have to be to become a complete player on and off the field and that's why he's a finalist," Baylor coach Art Briles said.

Then there was the Heisman Trophy, given to the nation's best player regardless of position. Stanford quarterback Andrew Luck had been the favorite, but as the season went on, more people started talking about Griffin. Baylor even promoted him with a web site, BU-RG3.com.

He had a chance to win one of the biggest honors in sports. He also had to decide if he would return for one more college season at Baylor, or go pro.

One outcome was not in his control. The other was. And in the end, the choice was easy.

Griffin became the first player from Baylor to win the Heisman Trophy in 2011.

MEMORIAL TROPHY

TO THE OUTSTANDING COLLEGE

IN THE UNITED STATES BY THE

Heisman and More

Why not wear red-and-white Superman-with-a-cape socks at one of the sports world's biggest events? It fit Griffin's personality, in part because he could do so many amazing things, and in part because, in so many ways, he was still a kid at heart.

He was at the Heisman Award ceremonies in New York City in December 2011. Andrew Luck was there. So were Alabama running back Trent Richardson, Wisconsin running back Montee Ball, and Louisiana State cornerback Tyrann Mathieu, the other Heisman finalists.

Then came the big announcement—Griffin had won with 405 first-place votes and 1,687 points to Luck's 247 votes and 1,407 points. He was Baylor's first Heisman Trophy winner. In fact, before him, Baylor had never had a player finish better than fourth in the Heisman voting, and that was in 1963.

"It was so well-deserved," Luck said. "It was very hard to be upset."

Griffin gave a memorable speech. He said:

Now that my socks are out there, I got nothing to lose, right? This moment right here, it's unbelievably believable. It's unbelievable because in the moment, we're all amazed when great things happen. It's believable because great things only happen with hard work. The great coach Art Briles always says great things only come with great effort, and we've certainly worked for this.

That's right, everybody associated with Baylor University has reason to celebrate tonight. To my teammates, I'd like to say thank you. As we say, the hotter the heat, the harder the steel. No pressure, no diamonds. We compete, we win. We are Baylor. Baylor we are, Baylor we'll always be, but it's up to us to define what that means, and this Heisman Trophy is only the beginning of that process.

To Baylor nation, I say this is a forever kind of moment, and may we be blessed to have many more like it in the future. God has a plan, and it's our job to fulfill it, and in this moment we have.

Griffin was honored for more than his football accomplishments. In just three years, he earned his degree in political science, with a grade point average of 3.67 on a 4.0 scale. He twice made the dean's list. By the time he left Baylor in spring 2012, he was well on his way to earning a master's degree in communications studies. Griffin had plans to go to law school.

As busy as he was with school and sports, Griffin spent a lot of time doing community service in the Waco area. He volunteered with Friends for Life to help senior citizens and disabled adults. He was a volunteer coach for the Special Olympics. He participated in a Waco elementary school reading program called One Book, One Waco. He also spoke to middle school and high school classes.

As busy as he was at Baylor, Griffin took time to make an impact in the community, including visiting children at nearby Cedar Ridge Elementary School.

"I think what I do the most is mentoring kids, and a lot of times it is people coming to me and asking me to talk," Griffin told *Baylor Magazine.* "I'm not one to turn a lot of people down. I sign a lot of autographs and do other things. You enjoy it while you can."

Because religion is so important to him, Griffin always celebrated scoring touchdowns by pointing to the sky to thank God. And because of his parents' military influence, he saluted teammates when they scored.

Soon he'd be saluting professional teammates. He would skip his last college season and enter the NFL draft.

While at Baylor, Griffin began dating a fellow student, Rebecca Liddicoat. They fell in love. Griffin proposed to her a few hours after leading Baylor to a 2010 homecoming victory over Kansas State. He proposed at the school's Allison Indoor Practice Facility in front of family and friends. With a teammate playing the guitar, he sang Rebecca a song he had written for that moment.

It was a big day in his life—but another was yet to come.

Griffin often likes to celebrate his touchdown runs with Washington fans by leaping into the stands during home games at FedEx Field.

A Rookie to Remember

Griffin started making money before he was drafted. In February 2012, Adidas signed him to a contract to promote the company's football, running, and training lines of clothing and shoes. Adidas officials liked him so much they paid as much as $120,000 to promote him on Twitter.

Soon companies such as Castrol Motor Oil, Subway, Gatorade, EvoShield (a body armor company), and Nissan signed him. Griffin even made the cover of Electronic Arts' *NCAA Football 13* video game.

Businesses liked him because he was great at acting in commercials. Before Griffin ever played in a regular-season game, he had made more in endorsements than any rookie in NFL history.

As far as the NFL draft, the Indianapolis Colts had the no. 1 pick. The Washington Redskins had traded with the St. Louis Rams to get the no. 2 pick, giving up three future first-round draft choices, plus a second-round pick. Both needed quarterbacks. One would take Andrew Luck. The other would take Griffin.

Two months before the April draft, he was tested by NFL teams and ran a 4.41-second 40-yard dash. He was as fast as, or even faster than, running backs and wide receivers.

On draft day in April 2012, the Colts picked Luck and the Redskins picked Griffin. They gave him no. 10, and his jersey quickly became the NFL's biggest seller. He signed a four-year contract worth $21.1 million that included a $13.8 million bonus. He made the rookie minimum of $390,000 in 2012.

The Redskins worked him in carefully during the preseason. He didn't play much and threw just 31 passes in the exhibition games. He didn't throw an interception, which was a good sign.

Griffin had one of the most impressive rookie quarterback first games in NFL history. He led Washington to a 40–32 upset victory in New Orleans against the Saints and superstar quarterback Drew Brees. He threw for 320 yards and two touchdowns. He rushed for 42 more yards.

It was the fourth-most passing yards ever for a rookie quarterback in his first start. Only Cam Newton, Otto Graham, and Ed Rubbert had done better. Griffin became the first rookie to ever win NFC offensive player of the week in his first week.

Griffin didn't slow down. He was named the NFL's offensive rookie of the month twice, in September and November 2012.

He had just the 59th perfect quarterback game in NFL history on November 18 against the Philadelphia Eagles. Griffin completed 14 of 15 passes for

Griffin was way too good for Philadelphia to handle in his first game against the Eagles. He only missed one pass and also rushed for 84 yards in one of the best quarterback performances in NFL history.

200 yards, four touchdowns, and no interceptions in a 31–6 victory, and again won NFC offensive player of the week. He and Drew Bledsoe are the only rookies to achieve perfect ratings.

To qualify for a perfect game, a quarterback must have a rating of 158.3. A quarterback must attempt at least 10 passes, have no interceptions, and complete at least 77.5 percent of his passes, with 11.875 percent going for touchdowns while averaging at least 12.5 yards per attempt.

Griffin hurts defenses as much with his legs as with his arm. He burned Minnesota for a 76-yard touchdown run in a 38–26 victory. However, he also suffered a slight concussion from a hit by the Atlanta Falcons.

Griffin and his family, including his fiancé, Rebecca, enjoy going out together. Sometimes, that even means the circus.

Washington coaches wanted him to be smart about running. They wanted him to use his mobility to get extra time for his receivers to get open rather than run and risk injury.

"It's almost scary to see how fast he's learning," coach Mike Shanahan said. "I've never seen anyone this young this good."

Then came his knee injury. Dr. James Andrews repaired the ligaments in Griffin's knee during a five-hour operation in early January 2013. Griffin tweeted his optimism: "Thank you for your prayers and support. I love God, my family, my team, the fans, & I love this game. See you guys next season."

The goal was to return as fast as Minnesota running back Adrian Peterson had. Peterson tore one of his knee ligaments in December 2011. He was back for the start of the 2012 season and rushed for more than 2,000 yards. Peterson gave Griffin his phone number if he wanted tips on how to rehab his knee.

"Yeah, Peterson is a freak [athlete], but Robert is a freak, too," Washington linebacker Lorenzo Alexander told *The Washington Post.*

When it was all over, Griffin won the NFL's offensive rookie of the year award. He had completed 65.6 percent of his passes for 3,200 yards, 20 touchdowns, and just five interceptions. He had a quarterback rating of 102.4, the third best in the NFL. He also rushed for 815 yards and seven touchdowns.

Griffin totaled 29 votes to beat out Indianapolis's Andrew Luck (11 votes) and Seattle quarterback Russell Wilson (10 votes) for the award.

"It's truly a blessing to be up here and be able to stand, first and foremost," Griffin said while accepting the award after his knee surgery. "It seems like the league's in good hands with the young quarterbacks."

It starts, and certainly doesn't end, with Robert Griffin III.

NFL Stats
Passing

Year	Team	G	Att	Comp	Pct	Att/G	Yds	Avg	Yds/G	TD	Int	Rate
2012	Washington Redskins	15	393	258	65.6	26.2	213.3	8.1	213.3	20	5	102.4
TOTAL	15	15	393	258	65.6	26.2	213.3	8.1	213.3	20	5	102.4

Rushing

Year	Team	G	Att	Att/G	Yds	Avg	Yds/G	TD	LNG	1st
2012	Washington Redskins	15	120	8.0	815	6.8	53.4	7	76T	40
TOTAL	15	15	120	8.0	815	6.8	53.4	7	76T	40

College Stats
Passing

Year	Team	G	Att	Comp	Pct	Yds	TD	Int	Rate
2008	Baylor	12	267	160	59.9	2091	15	3	142
2009	Baylor	3	69	45	65.2	481	4	0	142.9
2010	Baylor	13	454	304	67	3501	22	8	144.2
2011	Baylor	13	402	291	72.4	4293	37	6	189.5
TOTAL	15	41	1192	800	67.1	10,366	78	17	158.9

College Stats
Rushing

Year	Team	G	Att	Yds	Avg	TD
2008	Baylor	12	173	843	4.9	13
2009	Baylor	3	27	77	2.9	2
2010	Baylor	13	149	635	4.3	8
2011	Baylor	13	179	699	3.9	10
TOTAL	15	41	528	2,254	4.3	33

1990   Robert Griffin III is born February 12, in Okinawa, Japan.

1996   He and his sisters live with grandparents Mama Irene and John Ross, and great-grandma Evelyn in New Orleans while their parents are stationed in Korea.

1998   When his parents return, Griffin and his family settle in Copperas Cove, Texas.

2006   As a junior at Copperas Cove High School, Griffin throws for 2,001 yards and 25 touchdowns, and rushes for 876 yards and eight touchdowns.

2007   As a senior, he throws for 1,356 yards and 16 touchdowns, while rushing for 1,285 yards and 24 touchdowns. Griffin commits to Baylor University in December. He immediately graduates from Copperas Cove and enrolls at Baylor.

2008   In the spring, competing for Baylor, Griffin is ranked as the nation's no. 1 hurdler for 110 and 400 meters. He is named to *USA Today*'s All-USA Track and Field team. He wins the Big 12 offensive freshman of the year award in football that fall.

2009   Griffin hurts his knee in September and is out for the season.

2010   He graduates in December with a 3.67 GPA in political science. Griffin starts work on his master's degree in communications.

2011   He wins the Heisman Trophy. He is named college football player of the year, wins two national quarterback of the year awards (Davey O'Brien and Manning), and earns All-America honors.

2012   On January 12, Griffin declares he is skipping his last year of college to enter the NFL draft. In April, the Washington Redskins make him the no. 2 pick. On September 9, he makes his NFL debut against New Orleans, beating the Saints and veteran quarterback Drew Brees 40–32. Griffin is named to the NFL's Pro Bowl.

2013   On January 6, he reinjures his knee in a playoff game against Seattle. He has surgery to repair torn ligaments. In February, Griffin is named the NFL's offensive rookie of the year.

Works Consulted

"As Offensive Player of the Week, Griffin Provides a First." *The New York Times*, September 13, 2012. http://www.nytimes.com/2012/09/13/sports/football/nfl-roundup.html?_r=0

Atkin, Ross. "NFL 2012: A Banner Year for Rookie Quarterbacks." *The Christian Science Monitor*, September 9, 2012. http://www.csmonitor.com/USA/Sports/2012/0909/NFL-2012-a-banner-year-for-rookie-quarterbacks/Andrew-Luck-Indianapolis-Colts?nav=412094-csm_article-bottomRelated

Barra, Allen. "Robert Griffin III Takes Professional Football by Storm." *The Daily Beast*, December 3, 2012. http://www.thedailybeast.com/articles/2012/12/03/robert-griffin-iii-takes-professional-football-by-storm.html

"Doctors Optimistic After Surgery on RG3's Knee." *Herald Times*, January 9, 2013. http://www.heraldtimesonline.com/stories/2013/01/09/sports.788167.sto

"Dr. James Andrews Says He Never Cleared RG3 to Play after Injury, Contradicting Mike Shanahan." *Sports Illustrated*, January 6, 2013. http://tracking.si.com/2013/01/06/rg3-injury-james-andrews-knee-rg-iii-robert-griffin-redskins-mike-shanahan/

Hartstein, Larry. "RG3 to See Dr. James Andrews Again about Injured Knee." *CBSSports.com*, January 7, 2013. http://www.cbssports.com/nfl/blog/nfl-rapidreports/21511865/rgiii-to-see-dr-james-andrews-again-about-injured-knee

Jenkins, Sally. "Robert Griffin III: His Military Appreciation Will Play Well in the NFL and Would Benefit the Redskins." *The Washington Post*, March 11, 2012. http://www.washingtonpost.com/sports/redskins/robert-griffin-iii-poised-to-handle-the-pressure/2012/03/11/gIQAuOA45R_print.html

Jones, Mike. "Robert Griffin III Has 'Successful' Surgery on Two Knee Ligaments, Will Aim to Start 2013." *The Washington Post*, January 9, 2013. http://www.washingtonpost.com/sports/robert-griffin-iii-has-successful-surgery-on-two-knee-ligaments-will-aim-to-start-2013/2013/01/09/8f0d9f16-5aab-11e2-b8b2-0d18a64c8dfa_story.html

Judge, Clark. "Rivers on RG3: 'It's Always Easier to Ask These Questions Afterward.'" *CBSSports.com*, January 8, 2013. http://www.cbssports.com/nfl/blog/clark-judge/21520834/rivers-on-rg3-its-always-easier-to-ask-these-questions-afterward

Katzowitz, Josh. "RG3 Has Torn LCL, Will Undergo Surgery to Check His ACL." *CBSSports.com*, January 8, 2013. http://www.cbssports.com/nfl/blog/eye-on-football/21520825/rg3-has-torn-lcl-will-undergo-surgery-to-check-his-acl

Lewis, Ted. "NFL Draft: Robert Griffin III and Family Ties from New Orleans Are Poised to Celebrate." *The Times-Picayune*, April 26, 2012. http://www.nola.com/saints/index.ssf/2012/04/nfl_draft_robert_griffin_iii_a.html

Lucas, Paul. "Robert Griffin III's Historic Roman Conquest." *ESPN.com*, May 24, 2012. http://espn.go.com/blog/playbook/fandom/post/_/id/3023/robert-griffin-iiis-historic-roman-conquest

"NFL Rookie QB Roundup: Is Robert Griffin III Now Head of the Class?" *The Christian Science Monitor*, September 10, 2012. http://www.csmonitor.com/USA/Sports/2012/0910/NFL-rookie-QB-roundup-Is-Robert-Griffin-III-now-head-of-the-class/%28page%29/1

"RG3 Reinjures Right Knee in Fourth, Leaves Game." *CBSSports.com*, January 6, 2013. http://www.cbssports.com/nfl/story/21509074/rg3-reinjures-right-knee-in-fourth-leaves-game

"Robert Griffin III Heisman Finalist: RG3 Changed Baylor Perception." *The Huffington Post*, December 10, 2011. http://www.huffingtonpost.com/2011/12/10/robert-griffin-iii-heisman-finalist-rg3-baylor-football_n_1140784.html

"Robert Griffin III: 'My Relationship With God Is My Most Important Influence.'" *Black Christian News*, May 2012. http://www.blackchristiannews.com/news/2012/05/robert-griffin-iii-my-relationship-with-god-is-my-most-important-influence.html

Rosenthal, Gregg. "Dr. Andrews: Robert Griffin III Wants to Start Rehab Now." *NFL.com*, January 10, 2013. http://www.nfl.com/news/story/0ap1000000124563/article/dr-andrews-robert-griffin-iii-already-wants-to-start-rehab?campaign=Twitter_atl

Rovell, Darren. "RG3 Surpasses Luck in Early Endorsements." *ESPN.com*, August 25, 2012. http://espn.go.com/blog/playbook/dollars/post/_/id/1262/how-luck-rg3-match-up-in-endorsements

Russo, Ralph. "RG3 Wins First Heisman Trophy for Baylor." *Associated Press*, December 11, 2012.

Siemers, Erik. "Adidas Lands Heisman Winner RG3." *Business Journal*, February 21, 2012. http://www.bizjournals.com/portland/blog/2012/02/adidas-lands-heisman-winner-rg3.html?page=all

"Surgery on Redskins QB Griffin III Complete, LCL, ACL Repaired." *CBSSports.com,* January 9, 2013. http://www.cbssports.com/nfl/story/21525620/redskins-griffin-iii-has-surgery-to-repair-torn-lcl-examine-acl

"Transcript of Robert Griffin III's Heisman Speech." *BaylorFans.com.* http://www.baylorfans.com/forums/showthread.php?t=228309&page=1

Ubben, David. "Baylor Launches RG3 Heisman Website." *ESPN.com,* September 2, 2011. http://espn.go.com/blog/big12/post/_/id/32648/baylor-launches-rg3-heisman-website

"Unforgettable." *Baylor Magazine,* Winter 2011/2012, Vol. 10, Issue 2. http://www.baylor.edu/alumni/magazine/1002/news.php?action=story&story=105898

On the Internet

The Christian Science Monitor

> http://www.csmonitor.com/USA/Sports/2012/0910/NFL-rookie-QB-roundup-Is-Robert-Griffin-III-now-head-of-the-class/%28page%29/2

ESPN.com

> http://espn.go.com/blog/nfceast/post/_/id/43070/heres-a-whole-bunch-of-stuff-about-rg3

The New York Times

> http://www.nytimes.com/2012/09/13/sports/football/nfl-roundup.html?_r=0

GLOSSARY

AAU—Amateur Athletics Union; an organization that helps promote amateur sports.

humble—Being aware of one's faults.

hurdler—A track athlete who sprints over hurdles during a race.

interception—In football, a catch made by a defensive player when the pass was intended for a player on the other team.

ligament—One of the tough bands of tissue that connect bone to bone and help provide stability and strength.

NCAA—The National Collegiate Athletic Association; an organization that protects student athletes.

NFC—National Football Conference; one of the divisions in the NFL.

Olympic trials—A competition that determines which athletes qualify to play in the Olympic games.

orthopedic surgeon—A doctor who specializes in repairing injuries to or diseases of the joints, muscles, bones, tendons, ligaments, and nerves.

psychological counselor—A person who treats mental, emotional, and behavioral problems through talking with patients.

rehabilitation—A series of exercises and stretches designed to restore good health and performance.

sergeant—A rank in the military or police force that is above private and corporal, and below lieutenant.

Special Olympics—An international sports competition in which disabled athletes compete.

touchdown—Getting the ball into the end zone by a pass or a run, which results in earning six points and the chance to earn an extra point (for a total of seven points).